Alma Flor Ada

Authors *Kids Love*

An Author Kids Love

by Michelle Parker-Rock

Enslow Elementary

an imprint of

Enslow Publishers, Inc.

40 Industrial Road
Box 398
Berkeley Heights, NJ 07922
USA

http://www.enslow.com

This book is based on a live interview with Alma Flor Ada
on September 26, 2006.

*For my immigrant ancestors and my parents, thanks;
and for A.F.A., muchas gracias.*

Enslow Elementary, an imprint of Enslow Publishers, Inc.

Enslow Elementary® is a registered trademark of Enslow Publishers, Inc.

Library of Congress Cataloging-in-Publication Data

Parker-Rock, Michelle.
    Alma Flor Ada : an author kids love / Michelle Parker-Rock.
       p. cm. — (Authors kids love)
    Based on a live interview with Alma Flor Ada on September 26, 2006.
    Includes bibliographical references and index.
    Summary: "A short biography of author Alma Flor Ada, including her life, how she became an author, her books, and her advice to young writers"—Provided by publisher.
    ISBN-13: 978-0-7660-2760-2
    ISBN-10: 0-7660-2760-0
    1. Ada, Alma Flor—Juvenile literature. 2. Authors, American—20th century—Biography—Juvenile literature. 3. Cuban American women—Biography. 4. Ada, Alma Flor—Interviews—Juvenile literature. 5. Authors, American—20th century—Interviews—Juvenile literature. 6. Children's stories—Authorship—Juvenile literature. I. Title.
    PS3551.D22Z82 2008
    813'.54—dc22
    [B]   2008004641

Printed in the United States of America

10 9 8 7 6 5 4 3 2 1

To Our Readers: We have done our best to make sure that all Internet Addresses in this book were active and appropriate when we went to press. However, the author and publisher have no control over and assume no liability for the material available on those Internet sites or on other Web sites they may link to. Any comments or suggestions can be sent by e-mail to comments@enslow.com or to the address on the back cover.

♻ Enslow Publishers, Inc., is committed to printing our books on recycled paper. The paper in every book contains 10% to 30% post-consumer waste (PCW). The cover board on the outside of each book contains 100% PCW. Our goal is to do our part to help young people and the environment too!

Photo Credits: Courtesy of Alma Flor Ada, pp. 1, 3, 7, 11, 13, 14, 16, 18, 21, 22, 25, 28, 30, 32, 33, 47; Michelle Parker-Rock © 2006, pp. 4, 37, 40, 42, back cover; © 1995 Elizabeth Sayles, pp. 3, 8.

Cover Photos: Front cover, courtesy of Alma Flor Ada; back cover, Michelle Parker-Rock © 2006.

Contents

Author Alma Flor Ada at her desk.

A Book for Rosalma

One day in 1965, Alma Flor Ada was working on a book about creative writing for high school students. Rosalma, her four-year-old daughter, the eldest of Alma Flor's four children, was playing nearby.

My daughter was playing with paper and crayons and she said, "You haven't asked me what I'm doing." So I said, "Rosalma, what are you doing?" "I am writing a book," she answered. I said, "That's wonderful." "Why do you say that's wonderful?" replied Rosalma. "You haven't asked me why I'm writing a book." "So why are you writing a book?" I asked her. "Because," she said, "the books you make are so ugly!" For her, the high school textbooks I had written seemed unattractive, and she felt left out.

At the time, Alma Flor was living with her family in Winchester, Massachusetts, while working as a researcher at Harvard University. Up to that day, it had never occurred to Alma Flor to write a book for young children, but she wanted to compose something for her daughter. "I never thought of myself as a creative, inventive person," she said. "I thought that in order to write for children I had to be someone who was witty, funny, and exciting." For a while, she was unsure what to write and how to write it, but then she remembered all the stories and rhymes that she had treasured as a child. She rewrote the stories in her own words and put them together with some of her favorite childhood poems. When she read them to her daughter, Rosalma adored them, and her younger brothers, Alfonso, Miguel, and Gabriel, liked them too.

A year later, Alma Flor went to Peru, where she had gone to college. A company there agreed to publish her new book as a grade school reader. The book was called *Sonrisas*, which means "smiles" in

Spanish. It was a collection of retold stories as well as a few original stories written by a friend.

"My daughter loved it," she said.

By 1969, Alma Flor had developed an entire reading series called La Edad de Oro, which means "the golden age." She created collections of poetry, fables, folktales, biographies, riddles, and plays, and was involved in every aspect of the books' production, including the layout of the text and the art, as well as overseeing the printing process. Rosalma, Alfonso, Miguel, and Gabriel spent many hours with their mother in the print shop.

Alma Flor in 1965, about the time she started writing stories for young children.

It was a thrill for Alma Flor to know that children were enjoying her books. She said:

> On my long bus ride across the city of Lima, each afternoon I would see kids sitting on their doorsteps with these books in their hands.

In many cases, it was probably the only book they owned. I knew they were reading and rereading the book on their own because they wanted to. I was delighted to see that I had written a school reader they loved, as I had loved the books of my childhood. This led me to persuade the publisher to start a series of children's books.

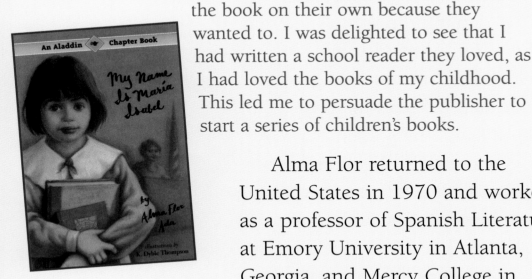

My Name Is María Isabel is one of Alma Flor Ada's most beloved books. It is enjoyed by readers of all backgrounds.

Alma Flor returned to the United States in 1970 and worked as a professor of Spanish Literature at Emory University in Atlanta, Georgia, and Mercy College in Detroit, Michigan. Within the next few years she was translating books from English to Spanish for a national publishing company.

By this time, Alma Flor knew that children liked her writing. However, she still did not believe that she had any original stories to tell. Then in 1975, she had an interesting experience while teaching a summer course at the University of Texas.

"I had eaten abundantly at the cafeteria," Alma

Flor confessed. "And I was thinking about how I had broken my diet once again."

On the way back to her room, it was very hot. Alma Flor felt like she was breathing fire. "All of a sudden I had an idea," she said. She wrote a story about a family of dragons that eats trains, buses, and planes—except for the mother dragon, who is on a diet and limits herself to eating station wagons. The story was published in a Spanish reading series that Alma Flor was working on.

"Once I had written this first completely original story," said Alma Flor, "I knew a door inside of me had opened. I have not stopped writing original stories, plays, and poetry ever since."

Alma Flor wrote a novel for young readers called *Encaje de piedra*, which means "stone lace," a mystery that takes place in the Middle Ages, during the building of a cathedral in Spain. The book was published in Argentina, and it won the Marta Salotti Gold Medal. "I love cathedrals, and it was a joy to write about something that had made a big impression on me," she said.

While teaching in Michigan, Alma Flor had met

several Latin American migrant farmers, workers who moved from job to job. After moving to California and becoming a professor at the University of San Francisco, she frequently visited with groups of workers to talk with them about their lives and their children. She said:

> In the summer, the workers sometimes worked in the fields until ten o'clock at night. One night, I had a late evening meeting with some parents. It was midnight by the time I was driving back home through the fields. I was thinking about the parents I had met and their generosity toward one another, when a story appeared in my mind. I could almost see it, as if it were a movie playing on my car's windshield. I was so moved, I cried all the way home. That night, I wrote it out. The next morning, I thought I had imagined it, but there it was on my desk.

Alma Flor took the story, *The Gold Coin*, with her when she went to Argentina to receive her medal for *Encaje de piedra*, and a publishing house there offered to publish it. When she got back to the United States, she shared the good news with her daughter.

Rosalma, now an adult, encouraged her mother to find a publisher in the United States instead. She thought her mother had written a story that children everywhere would love to read.

"I started sending my story out to American publishers and collecting the rejection letters I got back," said Alma Flor. The editors did not think that children in the United States would be interested in a story about a young thief determined to steal a gold coin from an old woman. "Every time it was rejected, I felt disappointed," she said. Rosalma continued to encourage her mother. Finally, in 1991, *The Gold Coin* was released in English by an American publisher. "The book won the Christopher Award," said Alma Flor, "and that opened the door for me to continue publishing."

Alma Flor with her four children: Alfonso, Rosalma, Miguel, and Gabriel. Grown now, all four children support their mother in her writing career.

Chapter 2

Stories With Soul

Alma Flor Ada was born on January 3, 1938, in Camagüey, Cuba. Her father, Modesto Arturo Ada Rey, was a teacher and a businessman. Her mother, Alma Lafuente Salvador, was an accountant who later became a teacher after coming to the United States.

Alma Flor grew up in La Quinta Simoni, a big old house on a farm outside of Camagüey. "Simoni is the name of the people who built the house and from whom my grandfather bought it," she said.

Alma Flor was very happy at La Quinta Simoni. "I was left to myself a lot of the time, and I spent many hours outdoors making friends with the trees.

La Quinta Simoni, where Alma Flor grew up.

I would sit on their roots, trace their bark with my fingertips, and talk to them."

Alma Flor's grandmother, Lola, would scoop her from bed while she was still sleeping and take her to where they kept the cows to get milk for breakfast. At night, her grandmother would rock her to sleep on the big front porch with brick arches.

"I would sit on her lap, and she would sing me songs and teach me poetry," said Alma Flor. "She'd tell me Greek myths and stories about Cuban history."

Alma Flor's father also told her made-up stories about the history of practical things, such as how people first came up with the idea of cooking meat or of covering their feet for protection.

My father loved solving problems. He could fix anything, build anything, and do anything that needed to be done. He enjoyed inventing these stories for me. He also taught me not to take things for granted. Even though I'm not mechanically inclined, I'm still intrigued by the world around me. Whenever I see anything new, I want to know who made it and how it works. When I go places, I'm observant. My father gave me that gift.

Alma Flor as a baby.

When Alma Flor looked out into the street in front of La Quinta Simoni, she often saw barefoot children dressed in rags, carrying big cans of water from the public water tap back to their homes. She knew that their mothers would use the water to wash clothes for other people.

> I knew how poor these people were. I felt guilty for having everything I had. I wanted to give them something, even though I knew it would never make up for how much was mine.

Alma Flor's most precious possession was a small iron stove with little cooking pots. It had belonged to her mother when she was a child.

> One day, I decided to leave the stove outside on the big porch. I had been giving all my toys away like this, one by one. Sure enough, within minutes the stove was gone. Later, when my mother asked me for it, I told her I had left it outside. My mother cried because that stove had meant so much to her. It was one of those moments when I realized how, in spite of my good intentions, my actions could have other effects, as well.

In *Pregones* ("the calls of street vendors"), a

Alma Flor playing with a dollhouse and toys made by her father. From an early age, she loved using her imagination.

collection of childhood memories, Alma Flor describes how her days were punctuated by the sounds of the people who sold their goods on the street. There were the baker, the milkman, the man who sold vegetables, and the man who came at night with the empanadas. Alma Flor said:

In the evenings, there was a man who came by with a big can. In the bottom of the can were warm coals and little empanadillas, half-moon pastries filled with either meat or guava paste. They smelled delicious.

Every night, my father would give me a Cuban coin that was worth about five cents. I would go out and buy two of the pastries for a nickel. My father, my mother, and I would share them. One night, I gave the man a nickel, but I told him I wanted two of the two-penny ones. Since they were two for a nickel, I figured one must cost three cents and the other one, two cents. I wanted two of the ones that cost two pennies each. The man looked at me, gave me two pastries, and gave me a penny back. I put the penny in my apron pocket and gave my parents the two pastries. I was so proud of myself and told my father what I did.

My father looked at me and said, "OK. What are you going to do with that penny?" I said, "Tomorrow, I'm going to buy cookies." My father then said, "What do you think a penny means to the empanada man? Do you realize he must live very far away from here? He walks every night carrying that heavy can. How many pennies do you think he takes back home? That is the money he makes and uses to feed his whole family."

My father didn't say, "You've done something wrong," or "You shouldn't have done that." He just shared his thoughts with me and left me with my penny. That penny burned a hole in my pocket the whole next day. I kept thinking and thinking about this man and his family. That evening, my father gave me a nickel and didn't say anything else. I went out and said, "Tonight I am buying two of the three-penny pastries." I gave the man the nickel and the penny. My father never told me what to do. He allowed me to experience my own feelings and invited me to reflect. This is how he taught me.

Alma Flor at about age three.

When Alma Flor was eight, her family moved to town and bought a gift shop. Her mother would often buy vegetables from a peddler who was Chinese. She always told the man that what he grew was wonderful. One day, the man said that something important was growing in China. Upon hearing that, Alma Flor pictured the willow trees and lotus flowers that were painted on the Chinese porcelain vases in the shop. One day, the man came with a young boy and said, "Here is what was growing in

China." Alma Flor realized that the man meant his son, and that he was not just a merchant, he was a father, too. She learned then that there was so much more to people than what they seemed to be at first.

She said:

> I never forgot that man. He walked those streets day after day with his heads of lettuce and bright red tomatoes, while his heart and mind were in China where his child was growing up. How could I not be aware of what it meant to be an immigrant, even though I had not lived that yet? I began to figure it out through that experience.

Alma Flor wrote about the street vendors of her childhood in a series of books called Cuentos con Alma. In Spanish, *cuentos* means "stories" and *alma* means "soul."

Chapter 3

The Cigar Factory Reader

Alma Flor's grandmother taught her to read when Alma Flor was just three.

She did not teach me with paper and pencil or a blackboard. She taught me out in the fields, by writing words with a stick on the ground. If we saw a cow, she would write the Spanish word for cow. One day she told my parents I knew how to read. They could not believe it. She had me read something, and my parents thought I had memorized it. So then my grandmother asked me to read some of the headlines from the newspaper. Next my mother gave me her own childhood copy of *Heidi*. It was a big red cloth book in Spanish. I read it and read it.

Alma Flor never stopped reading. "My parents were very generous. They bought me books, but not as many as I wanted." She often read the books she owned over and over again.

Alma Flor and her younger sister Flor Alma would act out the stories.

We would play all the different characters and do all of the things they did. I was probably nine or ten and my sister was two or three. We would pretend to be running away from wolves who were chasing us through the snow. We would cover ourselves with layers and layers of clothing and blankets, and yet we still shivered in the heat of the tropics. We were cold and shivering because the story was so powerful.

Alma Flor with her parents, Modesto Arturo Ada Rey and Alma Lafuente Salvador. A much-loved child, Alma Flor was raised with kindness.

21

Even as a young reader, Alma Flor enjoyed stories that offered different views of the world. She identified totally with the main character, Jo, in Louisa May Alcott's *Little Women*. "I could recite every chapter in that book by heart," she said. She also read *A Little Princess* by Frances Hodgson Burnett, *Tom Sawyer* and *Huckleberry Finn* by Mark Twain, as well as books by Charles Dickens and Jules Verne, all in very good Spanish translations.

Up until the time Alma Flor was ten years old, there were no public libraries in Camagüey. However, people could buy books and newspapers at one of two stores. One store had a soda fountain and was a good place to buy notebooks and pencils. Alma Flor said:

Alma Flor at age three or four, about the time her grandmother taught her to read.

You couldn't touch the books behind the counter. You had to ask to see one. Then, when I was ten, something wonderful happened. A United States Information Service Public Library opened, and I could just walk through the stacks and pull out the books.

Alma Flor would bring the books she was reading to her parents' store, which was also the office for her father's real estate and construction business and her mother's accounting work. Two young women worked in the shop. The days were long, but there were many hours when the store was not busy. During those times, Alma Flor would entertain the women, just like the cigar factory readers did in the Cuban cigar factories in the days before there was radio. It was tedious work to roll cigars all day by hand, so to make the day more interesting, the employees would pool their money and pay a person to read novels or newspapers to them. Although Alma Flor did not get paid to read, she enjoyed doing it.

> There was a little step stool that I would place behind the counter. I would sit on the stool and read my books aloud to the two women. My father would tease me and call me the cigar factory reader.

Chapter 4

The Playwright

"I was miserable in school until sixth grade," said Alma Flor. "When they put me in kindergarten, it felt like the room was much too small and my head was bumping up against the ceiling. It felt so confining to be indoors all day long."

For first and second grade, she went to an American bilingual school at the other end of town. She had to walk many blocks and take a streetcar to get there. Classes were taught in Spanish for half the day and in English for the other half. She was often reprimanded for reading the books that she kept in her desk.

In third grade, Alma Flor attended a different

American school because her parents wanted her to learn more English. This school was also located at the other end of town, and she had to ride the public bus.

> My father said I needed to learn to be independent. I was given two nickels and I would take the bus, which was never on time and was always very crowded. No matter how early I woke up, I was always late to school and was scolded every day. I was used to being treated kindly and so I didn't understand any of this.

Alma Flor at age eight with her baby sister, Flor Alma. As early as third grade, Alma Flor traveled a long way by herself to get to school.

Alma Flor learned how to do division from her father, who had been a math teacher. He taught her arithmetic the Cuban way, which was different from the American way. Although Alma Flor would get the right answers, when she showed the teacher her work, she was told she was not doing it correctly.

It made me feel so badly, because that was the way my father did it at home. That is why I understand so well how painful it is for children when they are taught not to speak the language that their parents speak. How could it be wrong to do something the way your father does it?

The experience made her unhappy, but she got good grades.

By fourth grade, Alma Flor's family had moved to the city, and her parents transferred her to a private Cuban school. "I was two years younger than the other kids, I was very small, and I was seated in the very last row behind some large boys," she said. "It was hard to even see the blackboard." The teacher would write long and complicated sentences on the board and then use them to teach grammar.

I could recite a whole book of poems, but analyzing those sentences did not mean anything to me. They were not even beautiful sentences. No one ever made connections between the course material and real life, so I felt very lost and frustrated.

Alma Flor remained at the Cuban school for

fifth grade, and in spite of all her struggles, she was a good student. "I worked my way up until I was sitting in the front row," she said. However, no one expected her nor encouraged her to do creative writing.

> My mother gave me beautiful notebooks to copy things in, so I copied poems and made my own poetry albums. She would also write some math problems in the notebooks for me to solve and show my father what I knew. Every year for Father's Day, the notebooks were my gift to him.

Then Alma Flor went to a public school for sixth grade.

> In Cuba, this was unheard of for a middle-class person, because public schools in Cuba were only for the very poor. Anyone who could afford to would send their child to private school. But my family knew the principal of the school as well as the sixth-grade teacher. This woman was extraordinary. So I attended that sixth-grade class. It was the first time I ever wrote.

It was also the first time Alma Flor saw a play. A major Spanish theater company had come to Camagüey. Her father decided to take her to see the performances. "It was an incredible cultural experience," she said. "I was completely taken by it. When I went to school, I couldn't stop talking about the plays I had seen." Her teacher suggested that they put on a play at school and that Alma Flor be the one to write it. "It was the first time in my life that anybody had invited me to write creatively, since we didn't do creative writing at school." Alma

Alma Flor at age fifteen.

Flor wrote the play and was cast in the lead role.

Alma Flor did not do any other creative writing until she was a senior in high school. It was a difficult year. There were many strikes against the Cuban government, which at the time was ruled by a dictator named Fulgencio Batista. In protest, people would stop working, and Alma Flor's school was often closed.

One of the history teachers decided to have us do projects instead of the usual lectures and exams. I came up with the idea of doing a historical play.

I didn't know anything about writing a stage play, so I made it up. We performed it in class and it was a great success. Then I wrote another one and we performed that one, too.

At the end of high school in 1955, when Alma Flor was seventeen, she wrote a third play, her first to be staged outside a classroom. It was called *The Sleepwalker*, and it took place in a boarding school for girls. It was a critique of the kind of education that is based on having students memorize large quantities of information. At the end of the show, the actors hosted a discussion about their high school experience. "Even then, I was already concerned about the process of teaching and learning," Alma Flor said.

In 1956, Alma Flor went to the United States for a year on a scholarship to attend Loretto Heights College in Denver, Colorado. Her parents thought it would be a good idea for her to spend a year there, learning more English, and then return home to attend the University of Cuba. Alma Flor was hired to help students with their Spanish pronunciation in the college's language laboratory. When the main

Book FACT

A Birthday Far from Home

Here is Alma Flor on her eighteenth birthday, at Loretto Heights College. It was Christmas vacation, yet she stayed at the college, almost the only girl there, since home was so far away. Her mother asked the sisters to celebrate her birthday, and they did so, in the Spanish classroom. "My mother had sent money for a cake and for a present: a portable typewriter—my best gift ever," Alma Flor said.

instructor became ill, she ended up teaching the course.

Upon her return to Camagüey, many people were still interested in her play.

> We rented a big theater in town, found props to create a set, and performed the show several times over the course of a few weekends. I was the writer, the director, and the producer, as well as an actor in the play.

Unable to enroll in the University of Cuba in Havana, which was closed because of the Batista dictatorship, Alma Flor went back to the United

States to attend another year of school, this time at Barry College in Miami, Florida. At that point, she decided that she wanted to study Spanish literature at a Spanish-speaking university. Her father sent her to Spain. Then her family left Cuba and moved to the United States. After two years in Spain, Alma Flor returned to Miami to be with her mother, who was expecting a child, Alma Flor's youngest sister, Lolita.

In 1960, Alma Flor was living in Peru, where she worked on a bilingual dictionary that was eventually published in the United States. However, she realized that what she really wanted to do was teach. She applied for a position as a Spanish instructor in the Abraham Lincoln Peruvian-American School. Alma Flor was much younger than the other applicants, and she did not have as much experience as they did. She also did not have an advanced degree.

> I did, however, have one thing to my advantage. I spoke English, and I could communicate with the principal of the school, who was American and did not speak much Spanish. That experience taught

me how important it
is to be able to speak many
languages.

Alma Flor at age
twenty, while she
was living in Spain.

She got the job and
continued working on her
own studies.

By 1965, Alma Flor
had earned a doctorate, the
highest college degree, in
Spanish Literature from
Pontifical Catholic University
in Peru. While working on
her doctorate, she taught in a
bilingual high school and wrote
and published several textbooks in Spanish. Not
long after, she received a special invitation to do
research at Harvard University, and she moved to
Belmont, Massachusetts.

After Harvard, Alma Flor returned to Peru
for two years and then went to Georgia to teach
at Emory University. Her mother was then living
in Georgia, teaching English to Spanish-speaking
adults.

My mother's students were Latinos from different countries. They knew that their own lives would never be much better. They were going to continue to work as janitors and cleaning ladies. Their hope was that their children were going to have a better life, and they were convinced that the key for that was education.

Alma Flor was worried that these parents' dreams for their children would not be supported by the school system. "I ended up leaving the field of literature and dedicating myself to education," she said.

Alma Flor with her mother, photographed in Georgia in 1965.

In 1973, she moved to Detroit to become a full professor at Mercy College. The bilingual movement was just beginning. "I wanted the college to know that I wasn't there just to teach Spanish and literature courses," she said. "I knew that I wanted to do something to help the Latino community." She began to develop a training program for bilingual teachers so that children could keep learning in their native language, while they were learning English as a second language.

> All children should have the opportunity to learn two or three languages when they are little. In Latin America and other parts of the world, bilingual schools are the schools of the elite, the people who have money and power and want their children to know other languages. I have no question that it is the best possible education for all children.

In 1978, Alma Flor went to work at the University of San Francisco in California. She was a professor there for twenty-nine years. She has dedicated herself to protecting the rights of all people to preserve their native language.

Hundreds of Books

Chapter 5

Alma Flor has written over two hundred children's books in both Spanish and English. She writes for many reasons: among them, to share her life stories and to preserve the moments she wants to remember. "The narratives in *Under the Royal Palms* are the memoirs of my life," she said. The book received the Pura Belpré Award, a prize given to Latino and Latina authors and illustrators whose work celebrates the Latino cultural experience. The short stories in *Where the Flame Trees Bloom* are also about her childhood. Alma Flor said many teachers use the book to motivate their students to write autobiographies.

"It is very moving for me to hear how much my readers have enjoyed reading about my life and the people in my family," she says.

Gathering the Sun is special to Alma Flor, because it recognizes the migrant worker's way of life. "The book was a way for me to talk about migrant farmers and the work that they do," she said. Many people have told her that they can see themselves and their families in the story. Some say they are sorry that their parents died before they could see their own lives in a book. "I think *Gathering the Sun* is one of my most significant books, because it is one that people treasure."

My Name Is María Isabel is another book that is dear to Alma Flor, because it addresses the meaning of identity. "My teacher insisted on calling me Alma, when my name is Alma Flor," she said. "It makes me feel good that many people are reading about how special names are."

Alma Flor loves to recite the award-winning *Lizard and the Sun*, a retelling of a folktale she heard as a child.

Alma Flor is especially proud of the Christopher Award she received for her book *The Gold Coin*.

The story stayed with me because I loved lizards. When I was growing up in Cuba, there were so many of them running around. I would collect their little eggs and place them in the ferns hoping to see one hatch, but I never did. I also admired the persistence of lizards, because that is part of who I am, too. I didn't give up. It is a meaningful story for me because of that message.

Alma Flor collaborated with her friend, author Isabel Campoy, to write *¡Pío Peep!* and *Mamá Goose*, collections of some of their favorite childhood nursery rhymes. In *Tales Our Abuelitas Told*, they share traditional stories that originated in Spain and Latin America.

I love folktales. They played a large part in my life when I was growing up. I love the stories of *Blanca Flor*, *Martina and Perez*, and *The Happy Man's Tunic*. My grandmother told me those stories, and I enjoy passing them on to others.

Alma Flor's Hidden Forest series came about when she was still teaching at the University of San Francisco. After teaching her courses, she would make a long drive to a small house she was renting north of the city. To keep herself alert during the trip, she would dictate notes to her students into a cassette recorder. "One night, I was tired of working, so I amused myself by imitating a pig, a rabbit, and a wolf," she said. "With the tape recorder running, I made up imaginary letters that these fairy-tale characters were sending to one another. I always loved letters, and I had a lot of fun with these." When Alma Flor got home, she put the tape aside without giving it any further thought. Sometime later, she listened to it and transcribed it. "I had completely forgotten what I had dictated on the tape," she said. "I was surprised to find a whole story there." The book, *Dear Peter Rabbit*, was the

Award-Winning Books

Alma Flor Ada's books have won many awards. Here are just a few of them:

Under the Royal Palms/Bajo las palmas reales
- Pura Belpré Award, American Library Association, 2000

Gathering the Sun
- Once Upon a World Children's Book Award, Simon Weisenthal Center, Museum of Tolerance, Los Angeles, California, 1998

The Lizard and the Sun/La lagartija y el sol
- Gold Medal, Folklore category, National Association of Parenting Publications, 1997

Mediopollito/Half-chicken
- Aesop Award Accolade from the American Folklore Association, 1997

Dear Peter Rabbit/Querido Pedrín
- Parents' Choice Honor Award, 1994

The Gold Coin/La moneda de oro
- Christopher Award, 1991

Encaje de piedra
- Marta Salotti Gold Medal, International Award for Children's Literature, Buenos Aires, Argentina, 1987

Other Awards and Honors
- Laureate, San Francisco Public Library, 2000
- Premio Mundial José Martí, Honors, San José, Costa Rica, for the overall contribution to children's literature, 1997
- Latina Writers Award, 1996

first in the Hidden Forest series. The next two books, *Yours Truly, Goldilocks* and *With Love, Little Red Hen*, are also told through letters exchanged by the characters.

For the fourth Hidden Forest book, *Extra! Extra!*, Alma Flor drew on her love for newspapers. Both of her grandfathers were journalists and owned papers in Cuba. The story is told in several editions of the *Hidden Forest News*. When a huge bean plant sprouts in Jack Blake's yard, some of the townspeople think it is a threat. Others see the value of its diversity and uniqueness.

Alma Flor with *Extra! Extra!*, the latest book in the Hidden Forest series.

Diversity is an important theme for Alma Flor. It encompasses her life's work. "I am very proud of this book," she said. "We must all learn to live in harmony with one another."

On Being a Writer

Alma Flor advises young writers to read whatever they like, but to read constantly. "I tell them to write and to trust themselves. It is essential for them to believe that what they have to say is valuable, that it is theirs, and that no one else can know it the way they do."

She reminds young writers that hundreds of stories have been written on the same few topics. For example, people have been writing about love, death, and family for a long time. However, Alma Flor believes that a writer can be original if he or she is truthful. "Try not to be concerned about what other people will think or how somebody else

41

Alma Flor stands next to just a few of the many books she has written for children.

would write it," she said. "Just ask yourself what it is you really want to say and write what is truly meaningful to you."

Alma Flor spends part of her time in northern California and the other part in Spain, where she has an apartment by the sea.

I do so many things, and I don't really have a daily schedule. When I'm home, I write on the computer. Some days I might write for eighteen hours straight, and the next day I might not write at all. I may just go walking in the woods instead. If I'm traveling, which I love to do, I don't stop writing. I just write very differently than when I'm home. I write longhand in notebooks that I carry around.

Most of Alma Flor's creative projects have emerged spontaneously. An example of this is

Abecedario de los animales ("animal ABC"), a collection of poems in Spanish. It is one of her most successful books. She said:

> I wrote that book because a very dear friend from Argentina came here visiting with her son. They were going to return to Argentina, and I was concerned that I might not see them again for a very long time. It was very important to me to spend time with her little boy, but I had a horrible cold and I couldn't get out of bed. I thought maybe I could write him one poem, maybe two. I wrote an entire book. The whole thing just poured out.

Similarly, Alma Flor wrote *Coral y espuma, Abecedario del mar* ("coral and foam, an ABC of the ocean"), while sitting on a beach in Maui, Hawaii.

However, when Alma Flor writes nonfiction books, she sets a schedule and sticks to it.

It took Alma Flor a long time before she thought of herself as an author. When she first heard someone refer to her that way, she said:

> I'm not an author. I've met authors for whom writing is all that they do, and they are highly professional about it. They keep up with all the latest news of the publishing business, and

are very aware of such things as awards and competitions. It has not been like that for me, because I have been so concerned about the struggle for educational opportunities for all. Sometimes it seems like a miracle to me that I have managed to publish as much as I have.

Alma Flor believes that to be an author is not primarily about the mechanics of writing, but about acknowledging that you have something to say. Once you recognize you have something valuable to communicate, you will find the right way to say it. What comes first is your ideas, your feelings, and your conviction that what you have to share is important.

Alma Flor said that she has always been trying to become a better person, searching for ways to become more understanding, more compassionate, more generous, more inclusive, and more responsive to others:

> At every step of the journey, whenever I have developed some degree of awareness, a story has come to me in one way or another, so that I could share that understanding with others.

Selected Books by Alma Flor Ada

Poetry and Songs
- *Abecedario de los animales*
- *A Chorus of Cultures*
- *Coral y espuma, Abecedario del mar*
- *Días y días de poesía*
- *El verde limón*
- *Gateways to the Sun/Puertas al sol* (series)
- *Gathering the Sun*
- *Gorrión, gorrión*
- *Música amiga* (series)

Nursery Rhymes and Folklore
- *Mamá Goose*
- *Merry Navidad*
- *¡Pío Peep!*

Narrative
- *Daniel's Mystery Egg*
- *Dear Peter Rabbit/Querido Pedrín*
- *Encaje de piedra*
- *Extra! Extra!*
- *Friend Frog*
- *The Gold Coin/La moneda de oro*
- *I Love Saturdays y domingos/Me encantan los Saturdays y domingos*
- *Jordi's Star*
- *The Lizard and the Sun/La lagartija y el sol*
- *The Malachite Palace*
- *My Name Is María Isabel/Me llamo María Isabel*
- *Stories for the Telling/Cuentos para contar* (series)
- *Stories the Year 'Round/Cuentos para todo el año* (series)
- *The Three Golden Oranges*
- *Under the Royal Palms/Bajo las palmas reales*
- *The Unicorn of the West/El unicornio del oeste*
- *Where the Flame Trees Bloom/Allá donde florecen los framboyanes*
- *With Love, Little Red Hen*
- *Yours Truly, Goldilocks*

Biographies
- *Smiles/Sonrisas*
- *Paths/Caminos*

abuelitas (ah-bwah-LEE-tahs)—Grandmothers.

abundantly—Fully.

bilingual—Speaking two languages.

dictatorship—A government that rules by force.

diversity—A variety of beliefs, ideas, and ways of doing things.

empanada (em-pah-NAH-da)—A pastry with a meat or fruit filling.

empanadilla (em-pah-nah-DEE-yah)—A little empanada.

grammar—A set of rules for writing and speaking.

guava—A tropical pear-shaped fruit.

immigrant—Someone who moves to a new country.

Latino—A person living in the United States whose family originated in Latin America or Spain.

migrant—A person who moves from one place to another for work.

pregones (pray-GON-ehs)—The calls of street vendors.

publisher—A person or company that produces books.

strike—To stop work to protest about something.

Books

Alma Flor Ada, *Under the Royal Palms: A Childhood in Cuba*. New York: Atheneum Books for Young Readers, 1998.

Alma Flor Ada, *Where the Flame Trees Bloom*. New York: Atheneum Books for Young Readers, 1994.

Internet Addresses

Alma Flor Ada's Web Site
<http://www.almaflorada.com>

Del Sol Books
<http://www.
  delsolbooks.com>

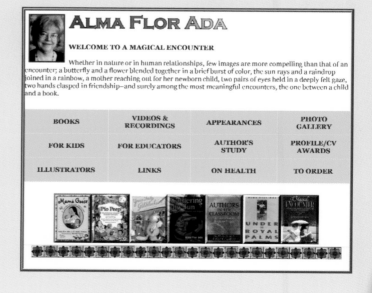

Index